Poetry to Soothe the Soul

Rebecca T. Urrutia

ELEVATION PRESS

Poetry to Soothe the Soul
By Rebecca T. Urrutia

Copyright © 2023 by Rebecca T. Urrutia

For more information, please see *About the Author* at the close of this book.

Cover photo by wirestock on Freepik.
Cover design and interior design and formatting by Elevation Press.

All rights reserved. No part of this publication may be reproduced, distributed, or transmitted in any form or by any means, including photocopying, recording, or other electronic or mechanical methods, without the prior written permission of the publisher, except in the case of brief quotations embodied in critical reviews and certain other noncommercial uses permitted by copyright law. For permission requests, write to the publisher, addressed "Attention: Permission Coordinator," at the address below:

Elevation Press
P.O. Box 603
Cedaredge, CO 81413

Ordering information: Quantity sales. Special discounts are available on quantity purchases by book clubs, corporations, associations, and others. For details, contact the publisher at the address above.

ISBN 978-0-932624-18-5

1. Main category— [Spiritual] 2. Other categories— [Meditation] — [Healing]

© 2023
Elevation Press
Cedaredge, Colorado
www.elevation-press-books.com

*This book of poems is dedicated to
the people who inspired me through my life-changing journey:
my family, friends, schoolmates, and Professors at Long Beach
City College—Robert Hersh, Cindy Frye, Sue Dittmar,
Ken Borges, E. Knorr, and Lisa Hopperton.*

My Heart Shines in the Mornings

Along the shoreline is where I like to walk
watching crimson and yellows illuminate the sky.

My heart eager
to see the morning light
and later the setting of the sun.

Each day I watch the seagulls flying above
and pelican's diving for food with such precision
the folding in of his wings
and the swirl just before the dive
makes me smile every time.

The large ships going out to sea
and I feel the swells come into the shore,
so soothing, harmonious, and vast is the sea.

And now I am composed, so I go on my way
I walk on and on and on to a new day.

Searching for Horizons

Yellows and blue of wondrous hues
came glimmering through the rain.

Which goes to show
there's still beauty
when we are in such pain.

And when you see
that all it is,
are illusions in your mind.
For then
you will see
that life can be
whatever you want to find.

Ember Nights

Reds and purples swirl in the sky.
The dawn of sunset has just passed by.
The wind hurls
against the trees
the illumination of hues
rage against the sea.
In only a moment
we can see
all the love casted
from each reverie.

Love in Nature

The songs of love are everywhere
you see it every day.
Open your heart and listen
you too, will see it displayed.
Bird's chirping is everywhere
and babies crying too.
You will see her love, as she tends the nest.
And yes, she does that too.
She hears their cry
and she is there
to feed and love them all.
And we have seen
and we learned
that love radiates around us all.

Streaming Dreams

There is a stream
where I like to dream.
Where butterflies flutter and float.
Where the river bends without an end
reaching for the stars.
While dancing through the endless night
the symphonies of my soul
take off in flight.

Forever Forgiving

Oh Jesus,
we ask that you forgive us today
for all that we did and did not mean to say.
And we know each day we must pray
to resolve all the things that lead us astray.
For today.
We ask that you strengthen our souls
help us to forgive and not to be cold.
Help us to love, to show others the way
like you did
on the cross
that day.

My Friend

My favorite thing is watching you
as you sit on my windowsill.

Your twitching nose and golden coat
gleams in the morning light.

I watch you
on your hind legs,
having your morning meal.
You look right into my eyes,
and I am deeply moved.

So precious is this sight, I smile ecstatically.

I wish everyone
would take the time
to see the beauty of the world.

To realize it is there for you
morning, noon, and night.

Nature and its treasures are found everywhere.
Just stop and look and you will see
there's magic in the air.

How can you say that there is no time?
when the morning has just arrived.

Open your heart and enjoy life
before your time has gone.

Miraculous Delight

There was a day when all was cold and black.
And I knew that I should not look back
for if I did the road would never end
and I desperately needed a friend.

I cried out, "Dear Lord, please help me now
I just do not know how."
His warmth glowed through me
and I felt delight.
For peace had come
through that glorious light.

April Showers

April showers bring us flowers.
As they bloom there will be no gloom.
For spring brings crispness to the air
of life, of love, of beauty to share.
To set us high upon a mountain stream
where we are left to dream.

Diamonds in the Sky

Oh Lord,
we see the glory
of the coming days.

Sparkling like diamonds
upon a moon haze.

Casting radiant colors
for all to see.
Letting us know
that love is
for all of us eternally.

True Treasures

If we can learn from our mistakes
how happy we will be.

For sad are those
who cannot see?

That life's true treasures
lie within thee.

The Ocean Front

The ocean is at my front door.
I go out every day.
I feel the ocean breezes brush my face,
and the rapturous warmth of the morning sun.
I see the water sparkling, so radiant is the sea
it reminds me of little fairies, dancing ecstatically.
Am I a child?
I am not.
The beauty in the world ignites my soul.

Try it my friend.
Walk along the ocean shore
and see what wonders you can explore.
I assure you, it will bring more peace and love
then you have ever had before.
Things money cannot buy, exhilaration, and much joy.

The Meaning of Life

What is the meaning of life, you ask?
I say to you, dear friend.
It is helping those in need today and
lending a helping hand.
The rewards are those of gratitude, love, and
the warmth of the soul.
We know these things are better than silver or gold.
The riches of the soul pay love to warm your heart.
So let your souls soar high above
while we ignite the sky.
Let us teach the world
to give with love and they will feel the joy.
And all we must do today is lend a helping hand.

Raging Sea

On a dark rainy day
we heard the roaring of the bay
crumbing ships, raging against rocks and land
trying to find a desert sand.
Until it's rage could go no more
a child came walking to the shore.

He cried out, "Please destroy no more."
I am awaiting my father
who is among the next roars?

Mothering Love

Among those laugh lines on your face
I see years of suffering, malice, and grace.
You took us in when we were young
not knowing where your meals
would come from.
You gave us shelter
clothing and a hope for life.
You taught us
to hold on with strife.
You showed us how to love again
until there be no end.
Your tenderness and love you shared
can never be compared.

Glimmering Star

Our souls
tell us
we were not born in vain.
For through life's trials
we have seen the rain.
Our love and faith
kept us on our way.
Knowing there is a purpose
in this world
that will soon be seen.
Of an unlimited love
for all
humanity.
And that
that star illuminating in the night
is our stairway
onto
the eternal flight.

Memories

Those sparkling eyes
shinning and glowing as a new day begun.

With precious moments
glimmering through one's mind.

Who could hardly forget?
of such wondrous times.

Children

They are a blessing, yes, they are.
So innocent and unsuspecting
are their souls;
so beautiful and joyful
in laughter
that warms our heart with gold.

Wish we could be that way, you say.
But we are
of the suspecting nature,
called experience,
who have witnessed the most
wicked of them all.

Our world is filled with many.
Some good,
some bad.
We must live here with them all.

I hope we extend to them this day,
the love
our children
have shown to us today.

Perhaps one day the world will change.
And finally,
see the light.

Your Love

Your love has brought
to me
in spring.

A life
So full of everything.

Grandma's Face

You are riding in a boat so leisurely
listening to the water ripple and the birds singing heavily.
The waterways lush with trees and flowers
the morning so lovely and crisp;
not a care in the world at this moment just laughter.
Young and beautiful with flawless skin
a smile that soothed even the crudest man.
Dreaming of life in another land
the journey was a difficult one
but sacrifice was a price for everyone.
Nothing in Arizona, so you moved on.
California was where you settled.
The years have passed and that beautiful flawless skin
has changed, showing suffering and tremendous grace.
My love for you will never change.
I see your smile and loving face
and once again I am renewed.

He is There for You

Our Lord has been there all along.
Why don't you call His name?

He is there to comfort and too soothe.
Why don't you call His name?

He listens and forgives.
Why don't you call His name?

He loves unconditionally.
Why don't you call His name?

There is nothing He will not forgive.
Why don't you call His name?

So, listen quietly as He calls
with love and open arms.

Dear child, I am here for you today.
To heal your broken heart
and guide you to the ascending light
where we will never part.

The Dawning Sunset

Her petals gently open
to the warmth of the morning sun.

With delightful breezes
floating through her hair.

Capturing dazzling prisms of golden light
radiantly glowing throughout the night.

Lady Liberty

In the eighteen hundreds we did not
have many rights.
In the nineteen eighties we took off in flight.
For our dreams, we have conquered.
We have seen the light.
Equality and freedom
are everyone's right.
So today
we salute
the Statue of Liberty.
For she is the symbol
of freedom in this land.
Where dreams come true
for one,
for all.
That is why she stands. So tall.

Soldier

You brought to me
so gallantly
a love to last
for all eternity.

Life's Trials

We wonder how we survive
in such a hatred world.
When people trample over others' needs
out of greed and pleasure
for thyself.
Where a baby cries his needs can't be met.
Our hearts weigh heavy
to all of this.
But our faith
tells us we were not born in vain.
That through our love
we shall conquer the rain.
And that
our Lord shall see us through.
For He is the one
who knows what to do.

Illusions

Has life ever seemed like an illusion to thee?
When all that we see
are things we have created to be.

Then if this, is it
surely it must seem.

That life was created,
for people to dream.

Sunsets

I go out each day
to watch the Sunset on the shore.

The sun is so huge
as it sets
upon the horizon's door.

So vivid are the colors,
as they explode.
Igniting the skies above.

Crimsons, yellows, blues, and pink
paint the sunset skies.

While my heart falls into ecstasy,
as you watch it here with me.

Love is in the Air

Do you see it?

Love is everywhere.
In the morning,
bustling streets,
where cafés are brewing
coffee.
And people smiling, everywhere.

The morning has brought
so much to see
in our little town square.
People holding hands,
men and women kissing
with hearts filled with glee.

Men whistling,
while people hum that tune.
Delightful is this day.

Birds singing,
so much music in the air.

And yes, you see
love is, everywhere.

Sedona

Sedona is my favorite place.
I feel so awesome here.
The vivid red rocks enchant me.
I feel so awesome here.
The wind roaring through the rocks, rage strange noises out to me.
I feel so awesome here.
The afternoon sun creates a hallway of light, filtering through the trees.
I feel so awesome here.
The art gallery creations are breathtaking and vivid and capture my soul.
I feel so awesome here.
While hiking at Boynton Canyon, I am enveloped by euphoria, which is magical.
I feel so awesome here.
The clear sparkling rivers and babbling brooks, resonate in my ears.
I feel so awesome here.
The rippling water and delicate sounds of the birds chirping, make this a haven.
I feel so awesome here.
The majestic mountains entice me, way beyond belief.
I feel so awesome here.
So, journey there my friend, and you will find.
That you will feel so awesome there.

Friends

Although the time has passed
our years have not elapsed.

Life's pangs we have beheld.
Which need not be told,
our friendship will never end.
I have found a dear friend.

Promised Land

We have all come to the promised land
overflowing with milk and honey.
Where dreams come true for one, for all
that is why
the Statue of Liberty
stands so tall.
For a man with a dream
encompasses visions of hope,
to work to feed his family is all he asks.
Whose endurance and hardship along the way
has taken a son fourteen
isn't that, too much to pay?
Then I say once more, please retake
your stand.
For, why are we here
if not to help our fellowman?

Rain

All I remember is what happened
in September.
When the leaves and the rain
caused so much pain.

Day by Day

Walking down the road day by day.
Trying to find a way, a way to say
life's too short for anyone to play.
When you lose yourself
there will be no way
to survive in a world
that rotates day by day.

Birds

Birds diving through the courtyard
so full of life and free.

To toss their wings from side to side
to love needlessly.

If only our lives
could be
so fancy-free.

Cranes

The beautiful cranes
so wild and free.

Gliding through life
in ecstasy.

Christmas Cheer

Christmas comes but once a year
with love
wishes of warmth and cheer.

Wishing you
a Merry Christmas
and tremendous
New Year.

The Bird of Paradise

The bird of paradise sees me now
but who could not?
If, he knew how.

This is Me

This is me
as casual as can be.

The flowers in the trees
remind me of what used to be.

Undying Love

Have you ever met a rich considerate man,
Whose warmth and kindness you did not understand?

For someone with success
you would not expect such a display.

Oh Lord, why
did we have to learn it this way?

Winds of Time

Winds of time blow through my mind.
The air so clean
Uh, so divine.
Pass through this set of time
onto an eternity of brine.

Pain

All I remember is what happened
in September.

When the leaves and the rain
caused so much pain.

The Fishing Village

This morning we are awakened
by the peeping sun.
Delightful are the breezes as they
fill our ocean shore.
Crashing waves roar out viciously.
While ocean breezes softly brush our face, as we walk out today.
Each day we come to hear the ocean roar and watch large ships
go out to sea.
The glimmering water enchants us as we feel that right away.
We tend to our day so eagerly and feel that all is good today.
Time has passed and with the setting of sun
we run out to see returning ships come into shore.
We say, who is safe today?
We thank the Lord for the returning men.
For He is the One who governs the seas.

The Hungry Children of this World

There are hungry children in this world today.
So sad and frail are they.

Our souls cry out to all of this.
For we have children too.

So, what can we do, you say?
Simple are the ways to donate what you can today.

Show others we can do something every day!

To heal and see them smile and laugh
will nourish our breaking hearts.

We will feel the light shine upon us, as we feel His radiant glow.

Our Lord is happy to see His children,
spread love around the world.

Winds

The wind blows clouds on into me,
like fog they cover and protect thee.

The chirpy birds so light and free
how come they never cry like me?

Through My Eyes

I start my day watching crimsons and yellows ignite the sky.
The colors so vivid as I see the morning light.

An artist's palette could not capture this, for
colors unimaginable have visited me today.

I wonder who it is that has shown this love for me.
For it is here today, so magically.

Fog

The fog's illusive mass.
Makes things look like the past.

About the Author

Poet and author, *Rebecca T. Urrutia* attended Long Beach City College in California where she earned her associate degree in Radio/TV Broadcasting/News and in Journalism with a Newspaper/Magazine Emphasis. She attributes her skills in Journalism to her instructor Cindy Frye and in Broadcasting to her professor Robert Hersh. Hersh is a four-time Emmy winner director in radio and television who received his second Emmy as an associate director for ABC'S *Wide World of Sports* in the 1984 Summer Olympics in Los Angeles.

The author's interests include archaeology, geology, astronomy, photography, art, and music. She also enjoys the ocean, aquatic animals, and past cultures.

As a child, Rebecca found it difficult to stay indoors. She loved the feeling of fresh air on her face and enjoyed watching the animals in her surroundings. She took a special interest in birds and squirrels, whose precious looks always caught her eye. In her later years, she found a fascination with spirituality and ancient cultures, as well as nature.

Writing about her life she recently observed, "I realized my creativity was emerging. I wrote from the heart and started with poetry. Analyzing life and conditions. I found my true passion in writing and started a collection of short stories in different genres. I am an explorer and hiker and have hiked extensively in Sedona, Arizona, and researched the Indigenous people who lived in the cliff dwellings. I also visited every cliff dwelling in Flagstaff, Sedona, Camp Verde, and Canyon de Chelly; it was amazing to see the structures still standing. Also, I have visited the Lowell Observatory in Flagstaff, Arizona. I had the opportunity to see Saturn from the Clark Telescope dome, an impressive sight."

Poetry to Soothe the Soul is her first poetry collection. She is also the author of a forthcoming children's book, *A Journey of Love with Baby Panda*.

www.ingramcontent.com/pod-product-compliance
Lightning Source LLC
Chambersburg PA
CBHW040555010526
44110CB00054B/2724